Before We Start

Scrum arguably is the most prominent agile framework used in today's development world. So much so that many people often synonymize agile with Scrum! Gone are the days when one needed to chalk out a detailed requirement plan months ago and developers had to follow that guide without caring for drastic market changes or the advent of new technologies. Scrum, like its other agile framework brethren, welcomes and accommodates changes - by breaking a large problem into smaller components and testing the features in the marketplace as much as possible through successive releases.

They say a picture speaks a thousand words. The motivation of writing this book is to regurgitate the core Scrum components through visual aids. The mnemonics will help you remember important Scrum concepts that are used in the present-day development process; bonus, if you are preparing for a Scrum certification such as Certified Scrum Master (CSM) or Professional Scrum Master (PSM 1), these pictures can help you greatly ace the exams.

This book can be best used as a supplement to the more formal Scrum papers or guides (e.g., Scrum Guide @ https://www.scrum.org/ – watch for the latest 2020 version). People who just started their career in a Scrum dominated environment may quickly get familiar with the important terms – everything is in pictures after all.

Contents

1. What is Scrum? 3

2. Scrum Artifacts 13

3. Scrum Players 21

4. Scrum Events. 33

What is Scrum?

A Framework

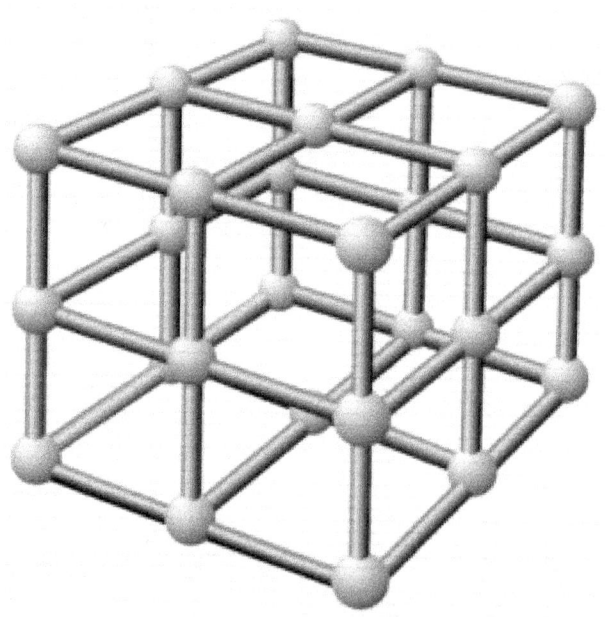

Small Team - Adaptive, Flexible, Feedback-driven

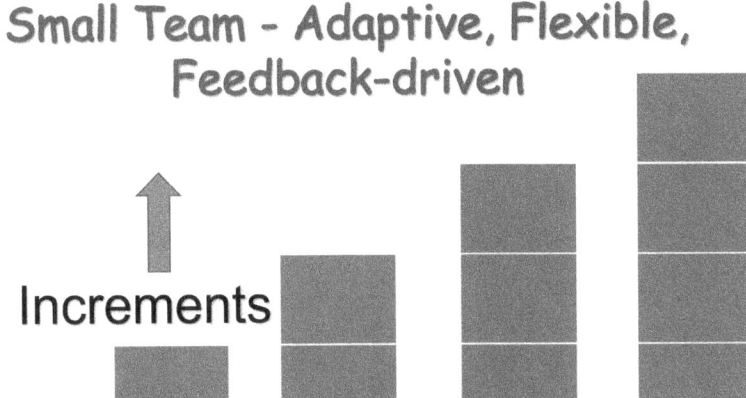

Increments

Iterations (Sprints) ➡

Scrum

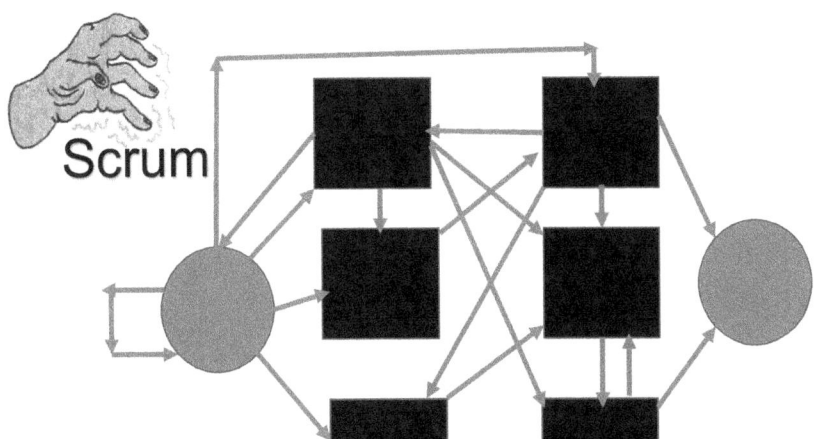

Can handle Complex Projects
Does it remove complexity altogether? NO !!

What Scrum Is Not?

NOT A Process OR Method

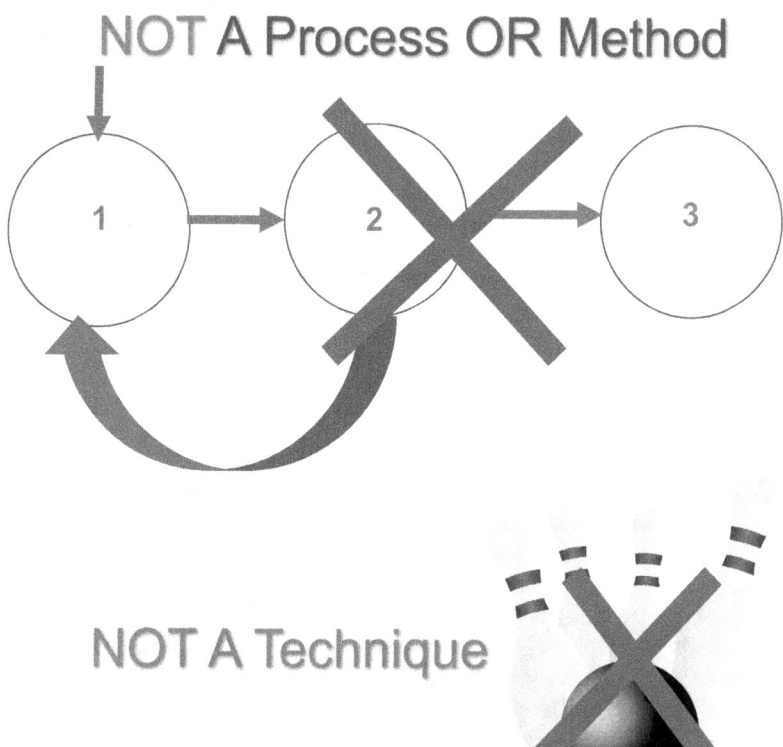

NOT A Technique

Then What It Is?

Lightweight

Can I reduce the # of Scrum
events & still call it Scrum?

An emphatic NO !!

BUT Hard to implement

Origin of Scrum (I)

Scrum Origin (II)

Reduce Waste Focus on Essentials

Lean Thinking

Scrum

Three Pillars of Scrum

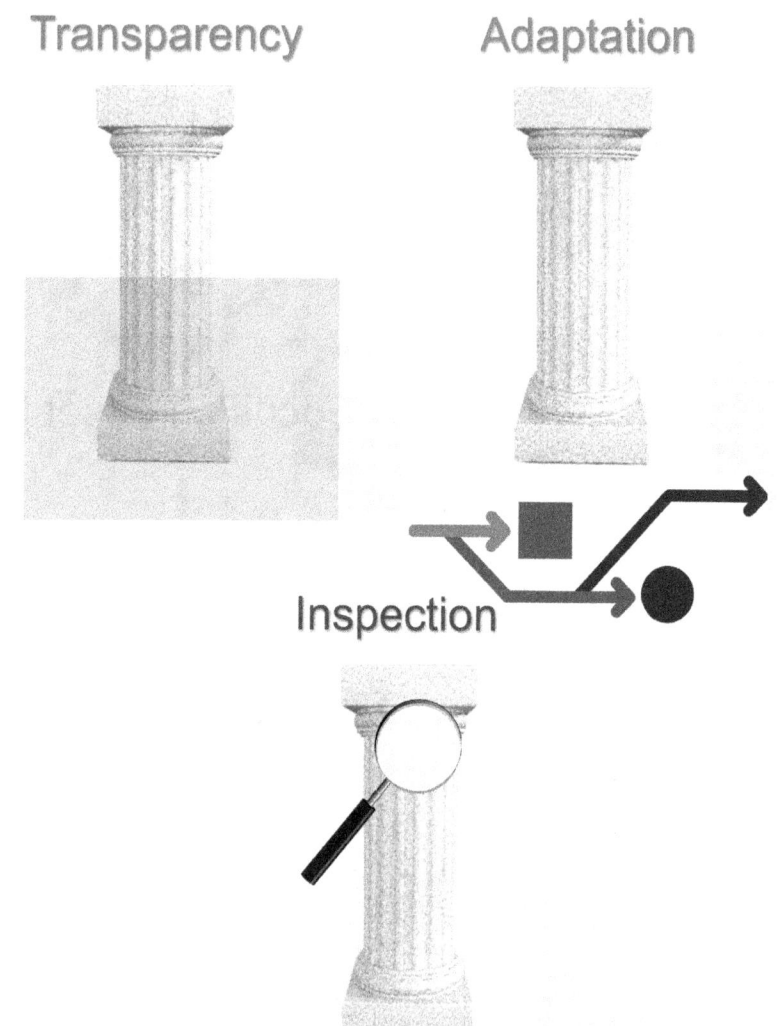

Transparency

Adaptation

Inspection

Scrum Values

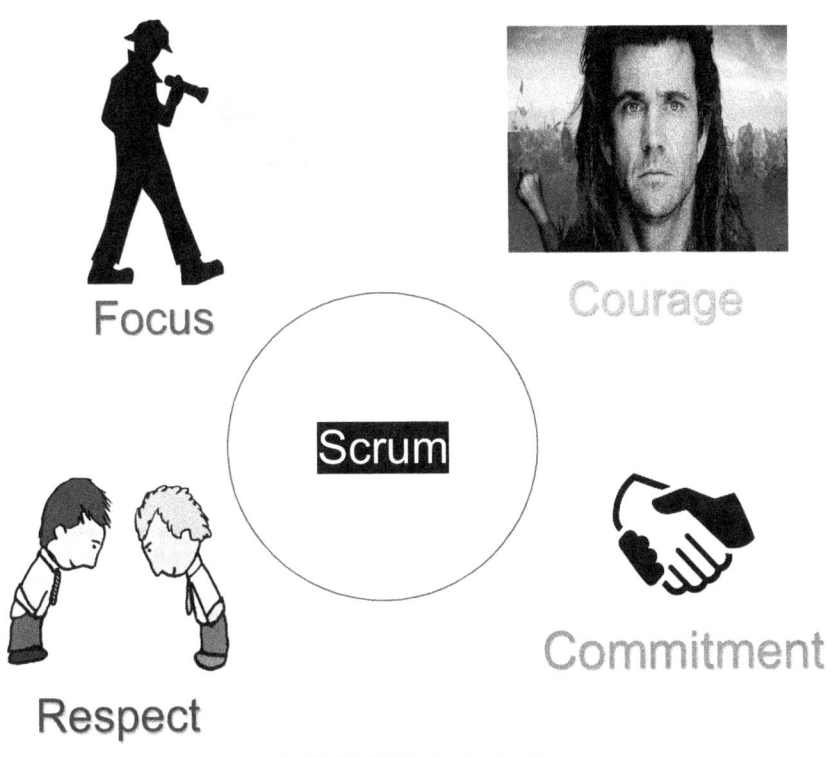

Focus

Courage

Scrum

Respect

Commitment

Openness

Scrum Components

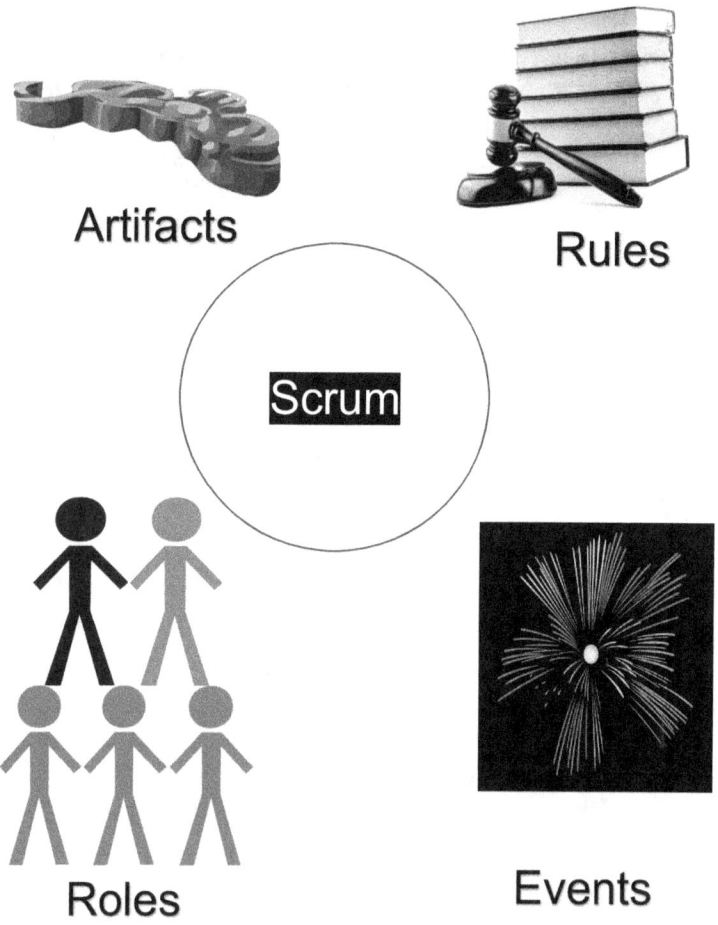

Artifacts

Rules

Scrum

Roles

Events

Scrum Artifacts

- **Product Backlog**
- **Sprint Backlog**
- **Increment**

Product Backlog
(1/Product, Tool for Transparency)

1. Pay button on Checkout tab is becoming inactive during tab switch.

   When a customer switches between the tabs and proceeds to pay through Credit card, she is unable to go forward. This has been happening in production since ~~August 23, 2020.~~ August 27, 2020.

Issue:	Defect	Status:	In Progress
Priority:	BP1	Assigned To:	John Doe
Story Points:	8 5	Sprint:	09/01

2. ....

Definition of Done
(Decided by Dev Team)

- Assessment   • Transparency

+ 80% test coverage
+ Completed requirement
  documentation
+ Completed code reviews

Sprint 1

Sprint 2

+ Met compliance standards
+ DoD-Sprint 1

+ Done Load Testing
+ 90% Maintainability Index
+ DoD-Sprint 2

Sprint 3

Producing Increments (I)

Product Backlog: managed by PO

1. .....
2. .....
3. .....

51.....

Clarity,
Value

Sprint Backlogs: managed by Dev Team

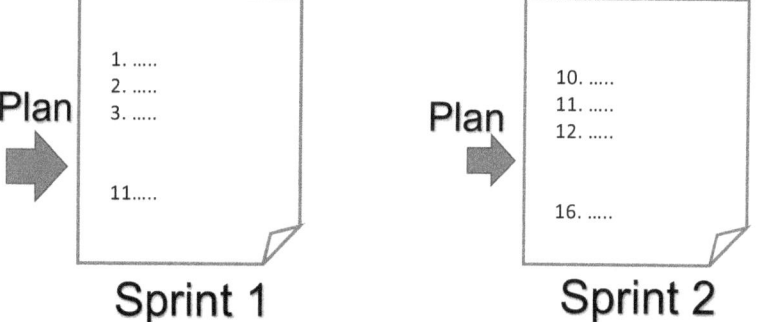

Plan

1. .....
2. .....
3. .....

11.....

Plan

10. .....
11. .....
12. .....

16. .....

Sprint 1   Sprint 2

Increments: produced by Dev Team

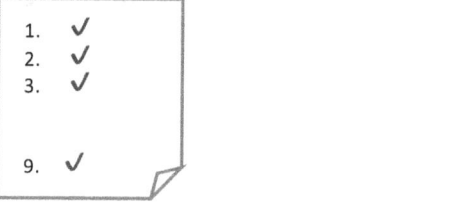

1. ✓
2. ✓
3. ✓

9. ✓

10. ✓
11. ✓
12. ✓

16. ✓

Producing Increments (II)

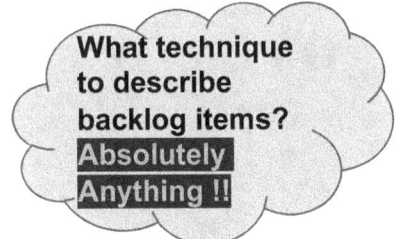

Product Backlog Items

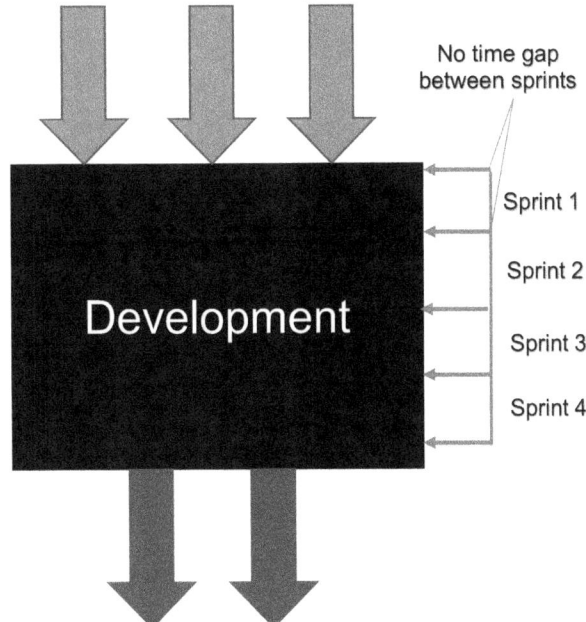

Releasable Increments
(Done items + Earlier increments)

Product Backlog Refinement
(PO + Dev Team)

☑ An ongoing process

☑ Should NOT consume much development capacity (<10%)

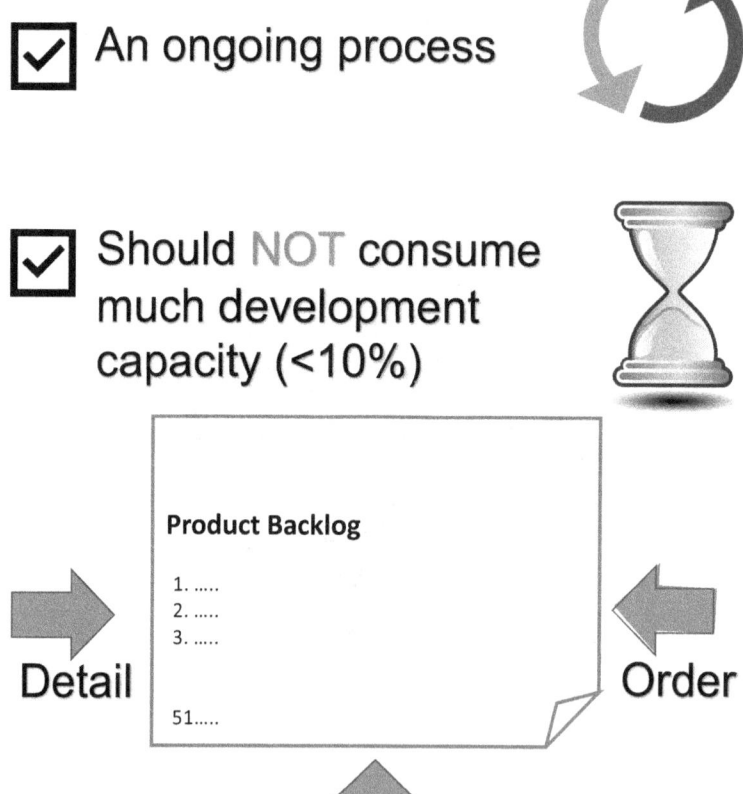

Product Backlog

1. .....
2. .....
3. .....

51.....

Detail

Order

Estimate
(ONLY Dev Team has the expertise to provide an effort number)

Cone of Uncertainty

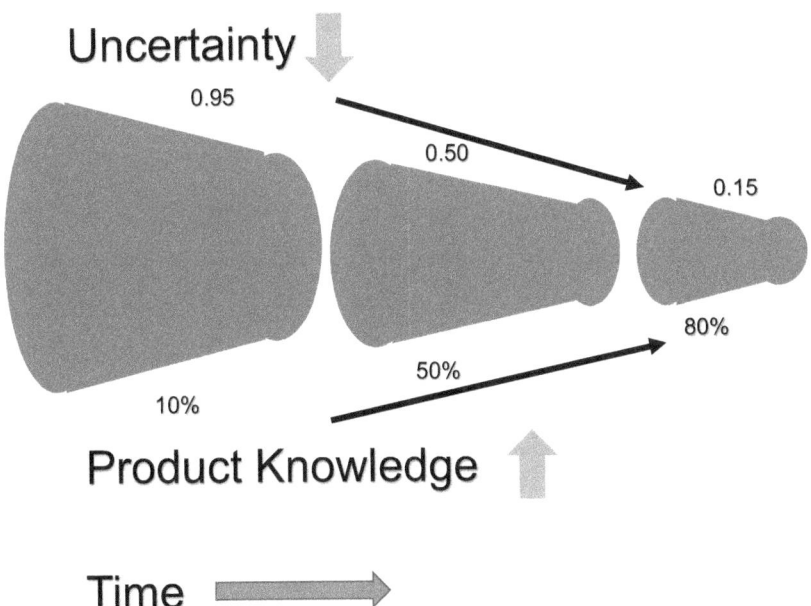

Uncertainty

0.95

0.50

0.15

10%

50%

80%

Product Knowledge

Time

Optimization Factors

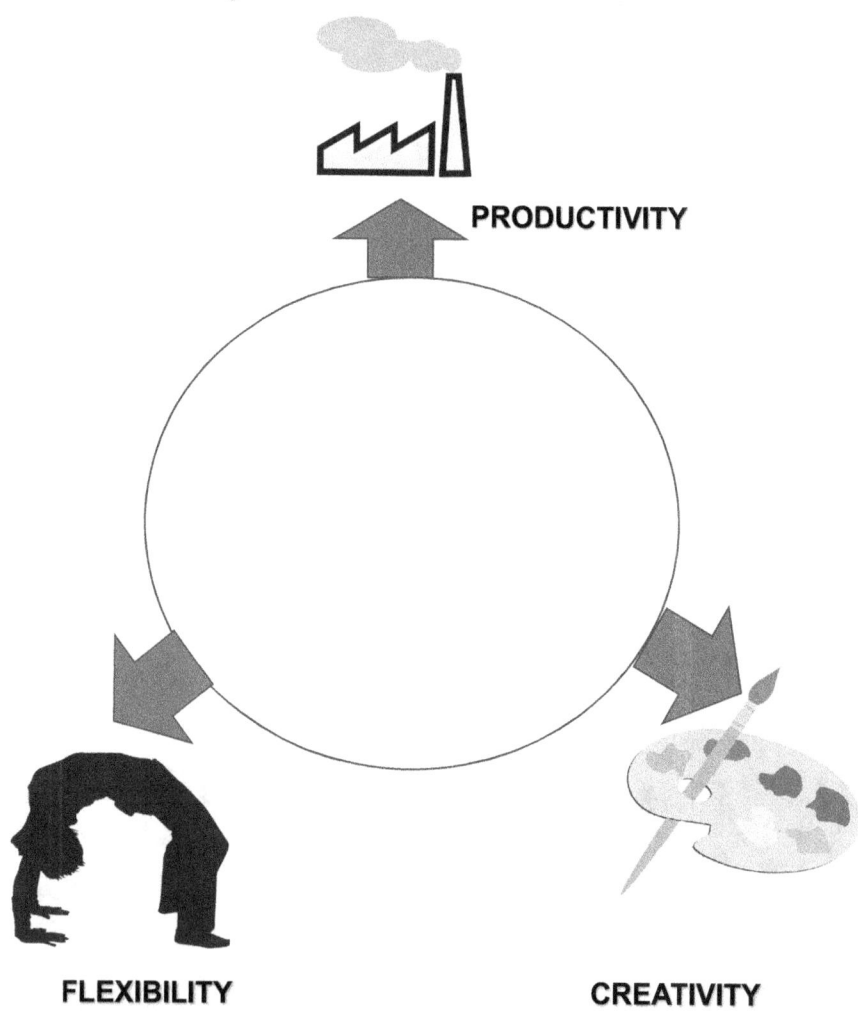

PRODUCTIVITY

FLEXIBILITY

CREATIVITY

Scrum Players

- **Product Owner (+)**
- **Scrum Master (+)**
- **Development Team (+)**

- Executives
- Management
- Domain Experts
- Shareholders

Team Composition

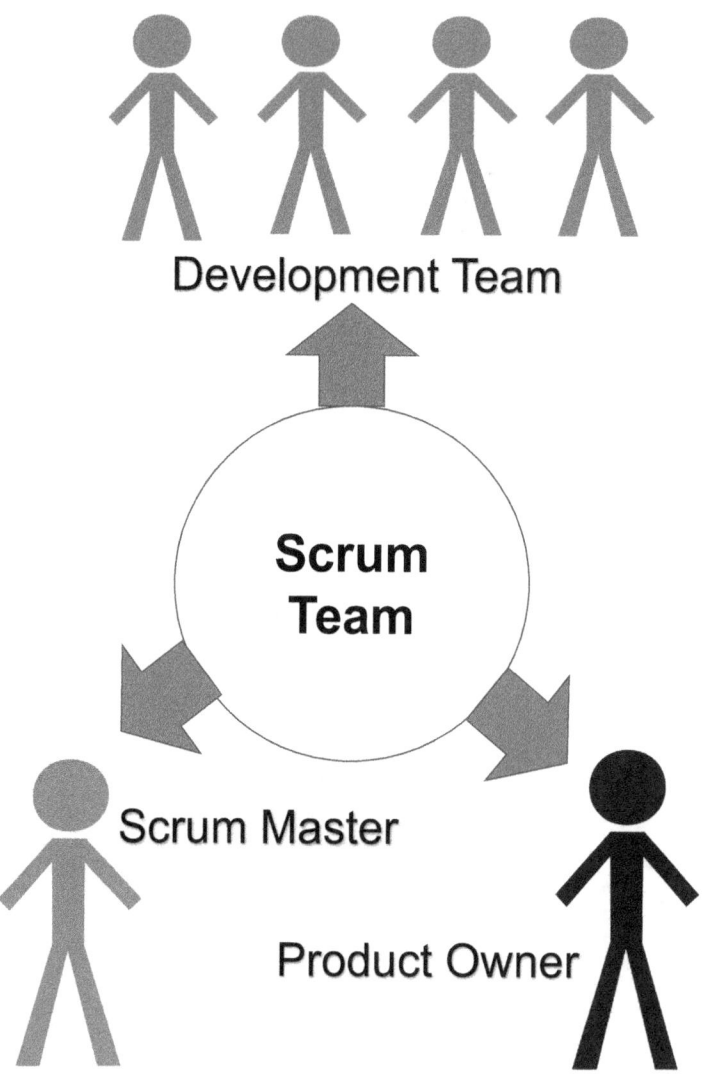

Development Team

Scrum
Team

Scrum Master

Product Owner

NO Project Manager, Engineering Manager, Architect/ Team Lead Roles

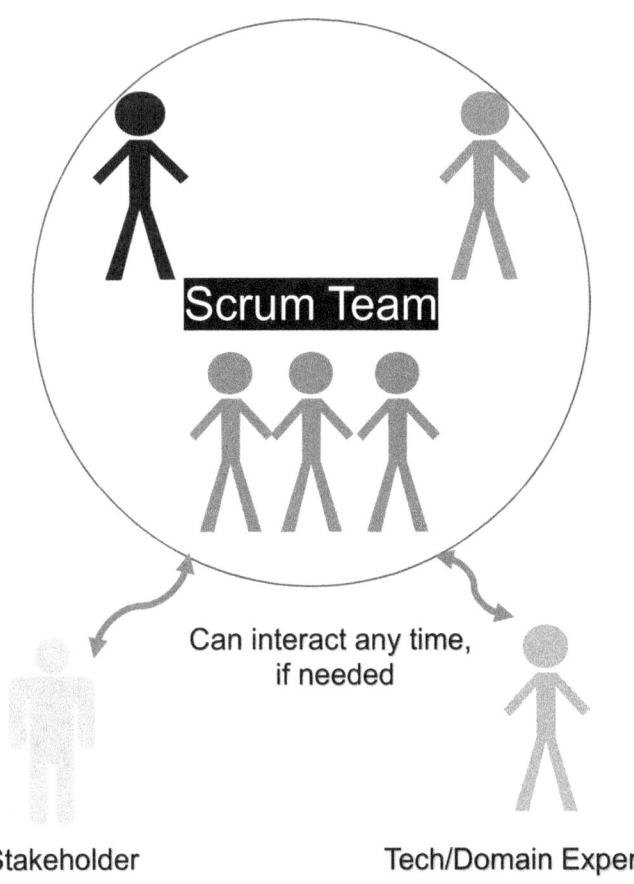

Scrum Team

Can interact any time, if needed

Stakeholder

Tech/Domain Expert
(External)

Product Owner: Chief Product Visionary

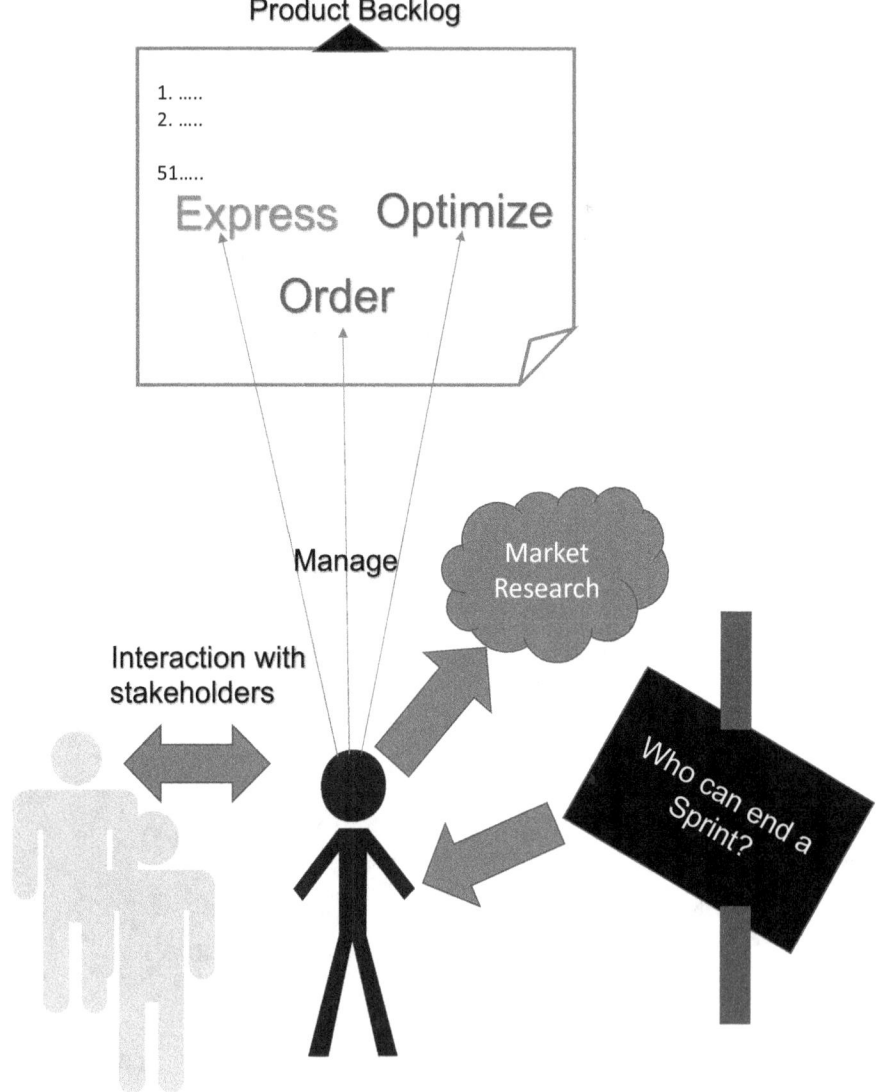

Factors to Consider Before Release

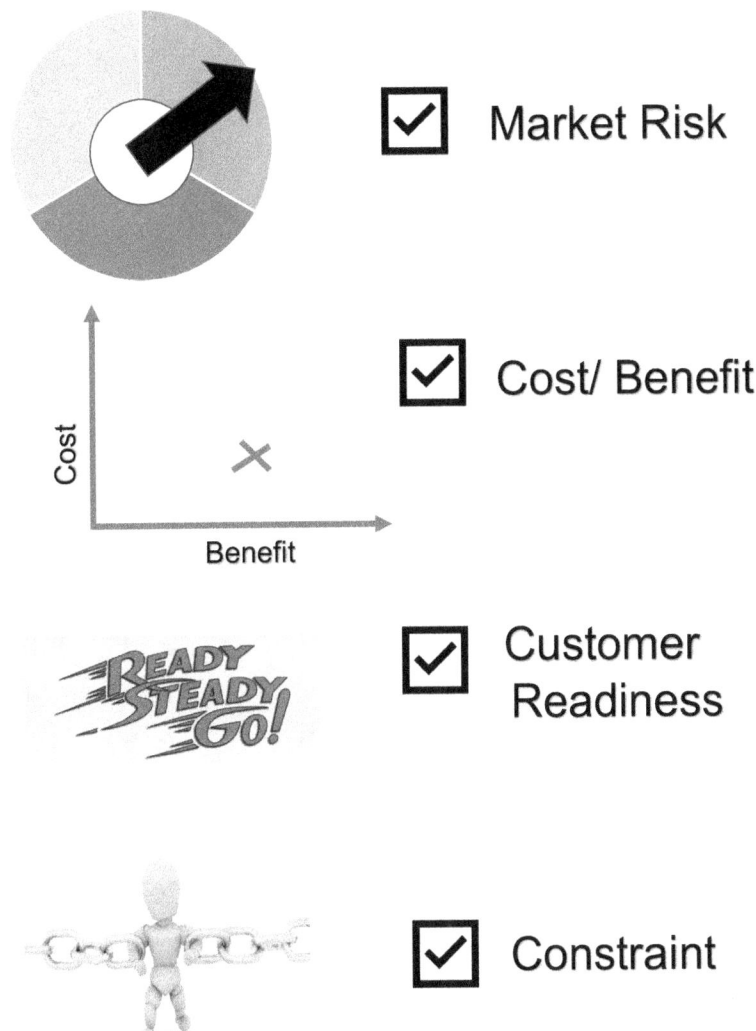

☑ Market Risk

☑ Cost/ Benefit

☑ Customer Readiness

☑ Constraint

Scrum Master
Scrum Champion & Coordinator

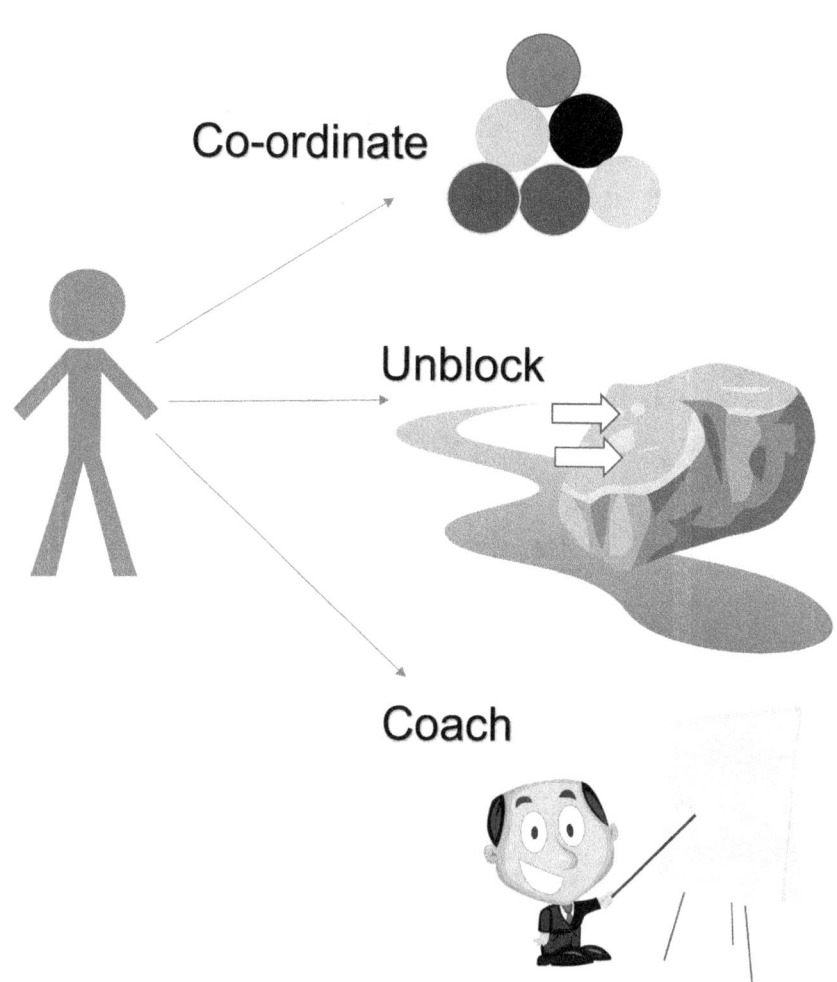

Co-ordinate

Unblock

Coach

Scrum Master To Product Owner

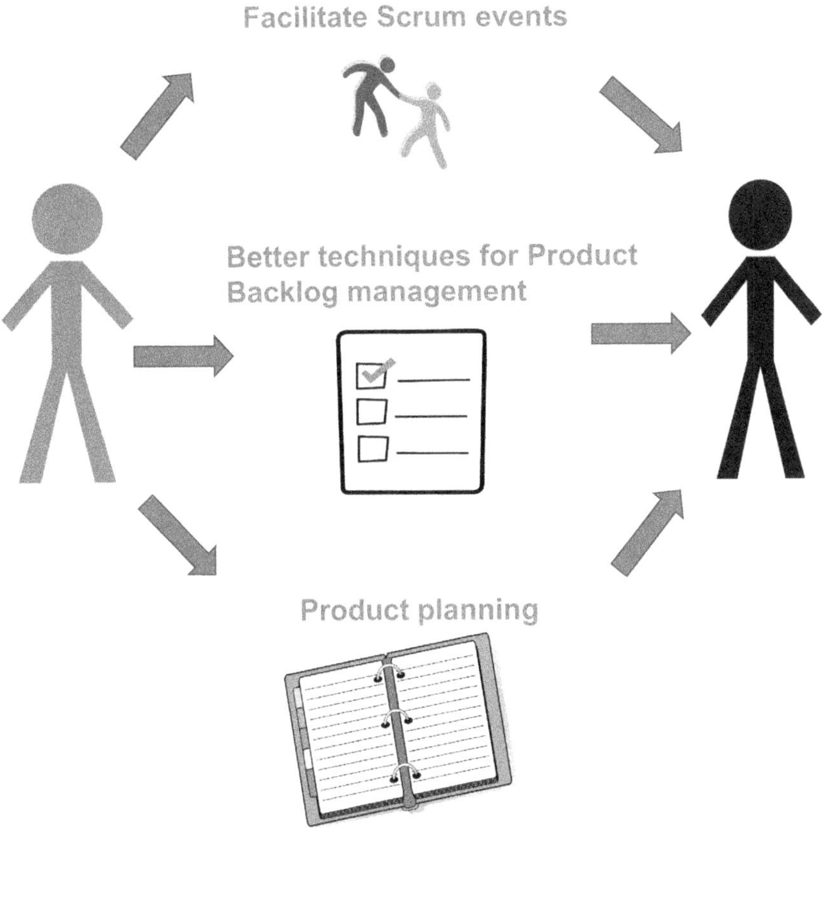

Facilitate Scrum events

Better techniques for Product Backlog management

Product planning

Scrum Master To Daily Scrum

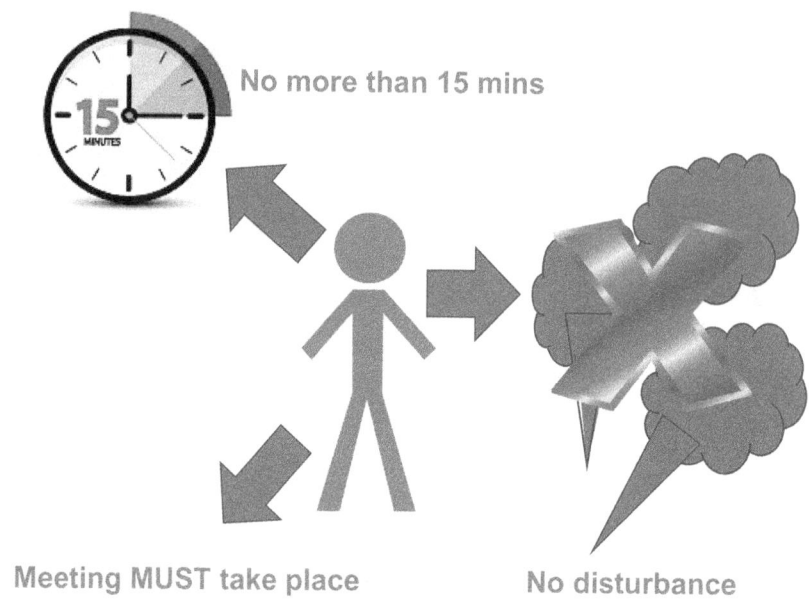

No more than 15 mins

Meeting MUST take place

No disturbance

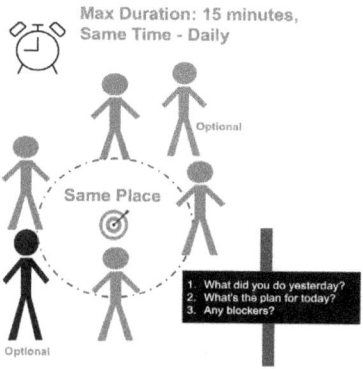

Max Duration: 15 minutes, Same Time - Daily

Optional

Same Place

Optional

1. What did you do yesterday?
2. What's the plan for today?
3. Any blockers?

Development Team (I)

3<=Team Size<=9

Too Few!

Too Many!!

Development Team (II)

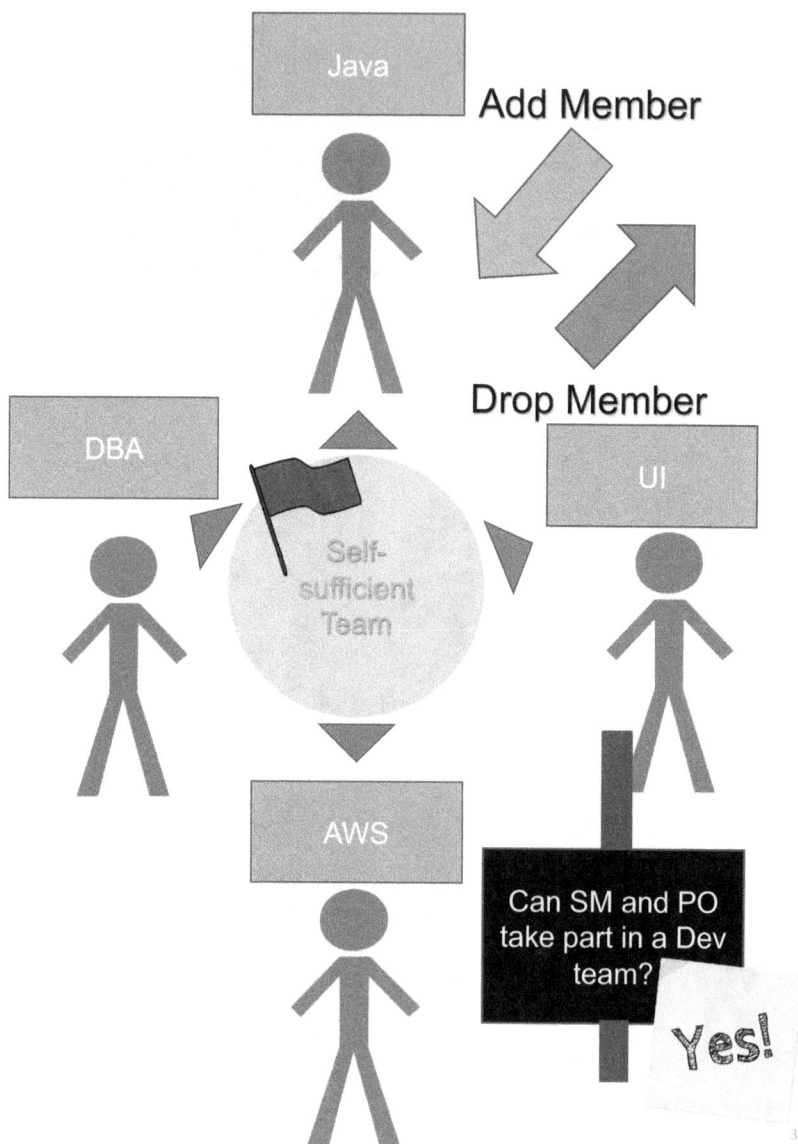

Management/ Executives

Product Owner

Scrum Master

Info about Product & Capability

Support for Scrum

Who Are Stakeholders?

  User

  Payer

  Funding Sponsor

Scrum Events

Formal Inspect & Adapt

Timebox- A Strict Upper Limit

Event boundary: max time an event can span

Sprint Length
(1 month? 2 weeks? 1 week?)

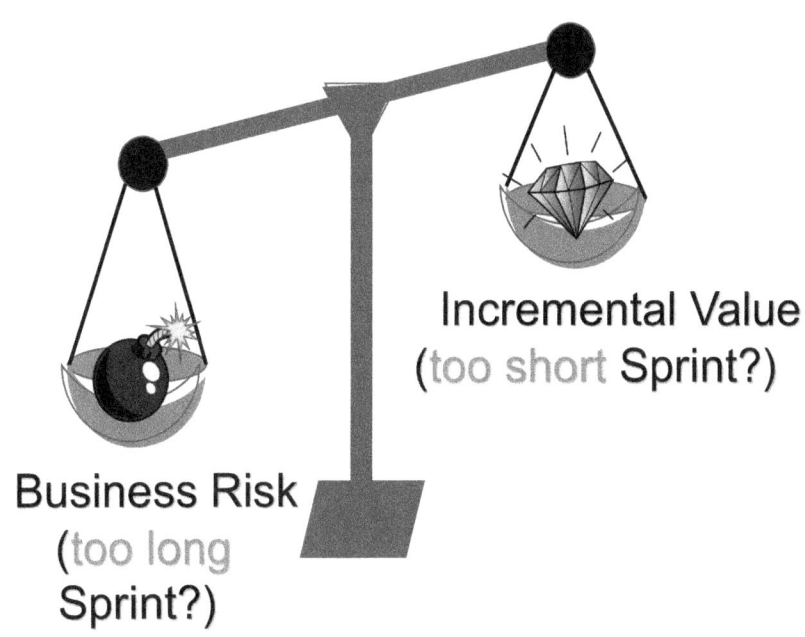

Incremental Value
(too short Sprint?)

Business Risk
(too long
Sprint?)

Sprint Planning (I)

 Max Duration: 8 hours

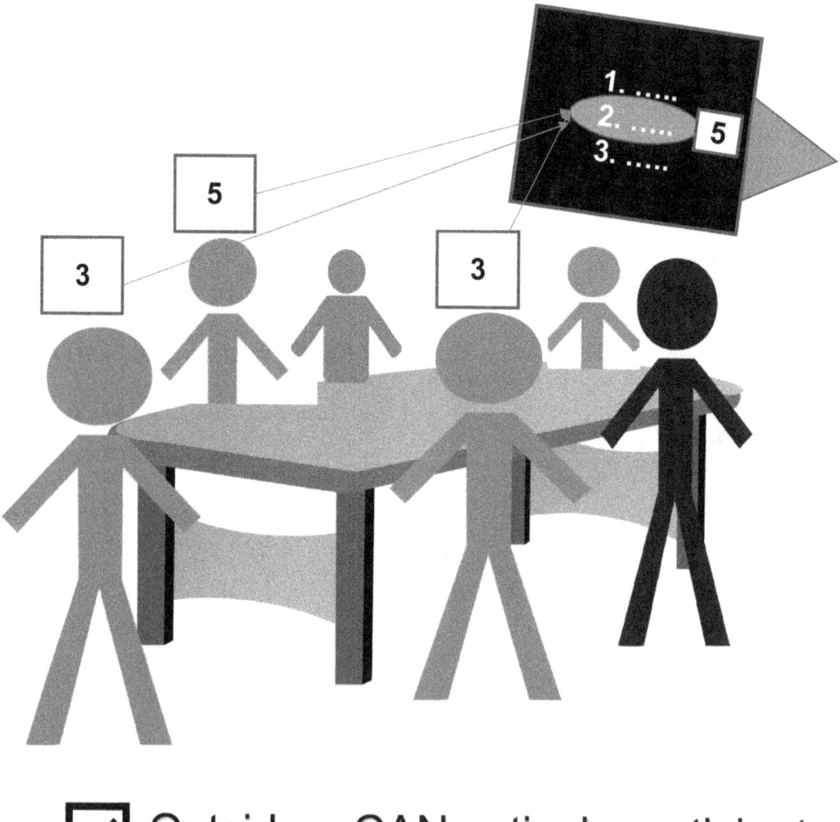

☑ Outsiders CAN actively participate

Sprint Planning (II)

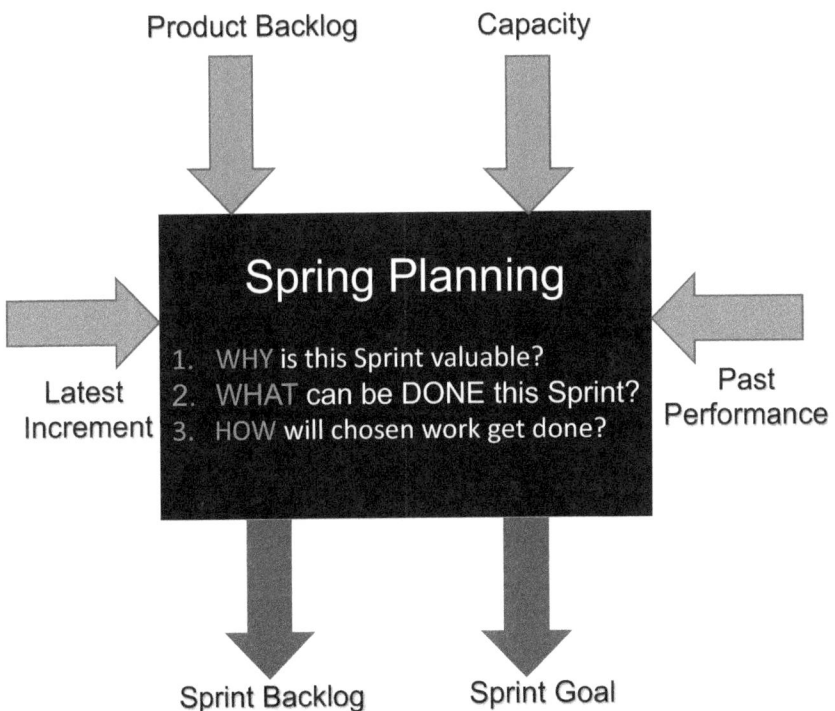

Daily Scrum

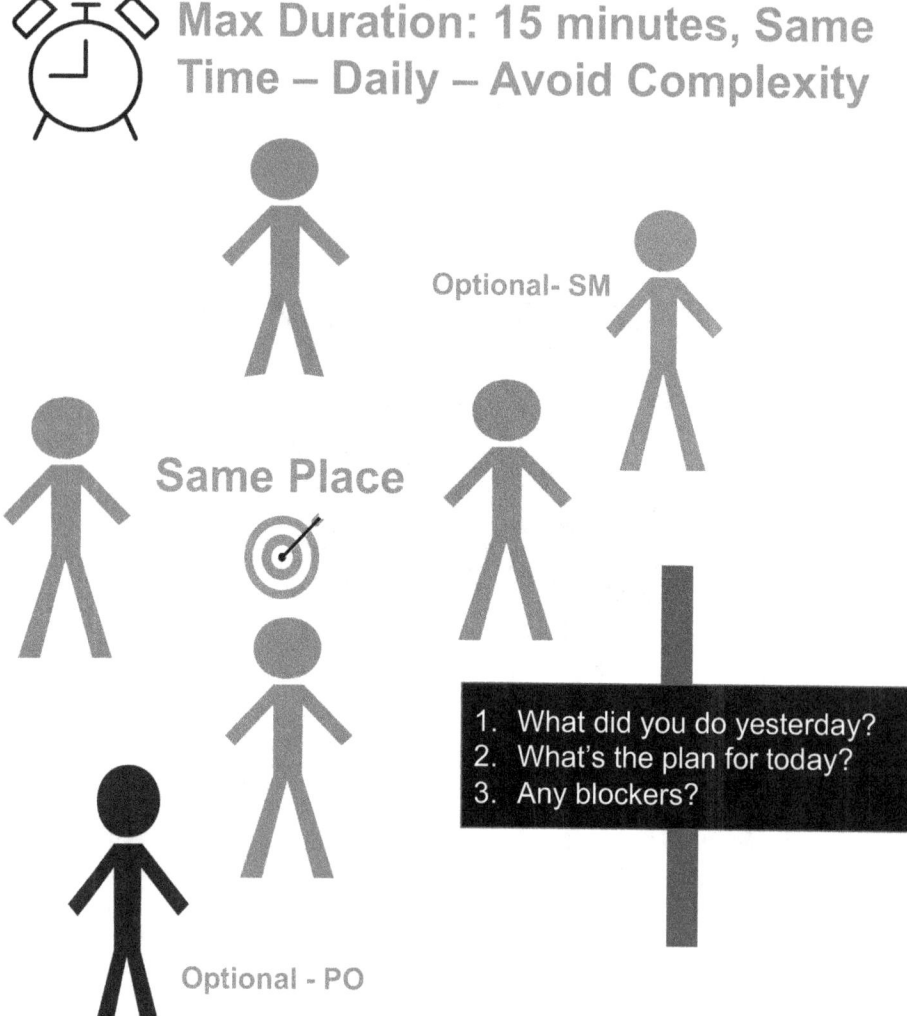

Max Duration: 15 minutes, Same Time – Daily – Avoid Complexity

Optional- SM

Same Place

1. What did you do yesterday?
2. What's the plan for today?
3. Any blockers?

Optional - PO

Sprint Review

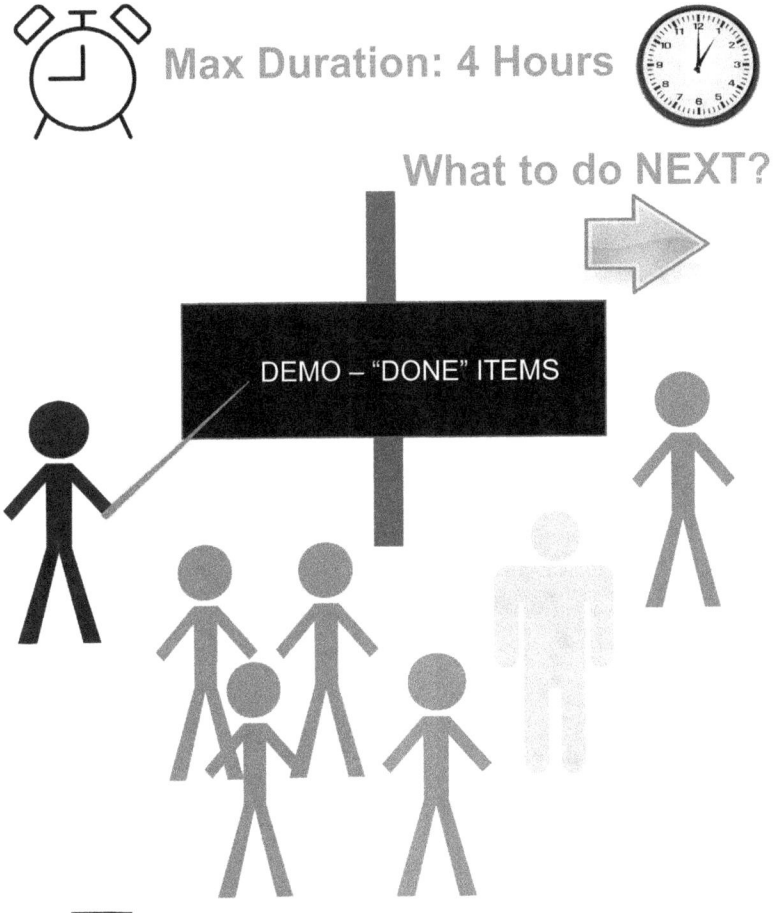

Max Duration: 4 Hours

What to do NEXT?

DEMO – "DONE" ITEMS

☑ Outsiders CAN actively participate

Sprint Retrospective (Inspect and Improve)

 Max Duration: 3 hours

How did last sprint go?

What went well?

Plan for future sprints

Sprint Cancellation: By Product Owner

Sprint goal becomes obsolete

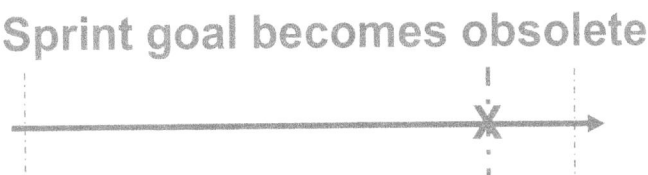

What to do after Sprint cancellation?

Sprint Backlog Items

PB ←	Incomplete	"Done"	Potentially Releasable	→ Release

↓

Review

Tools to Track Progress

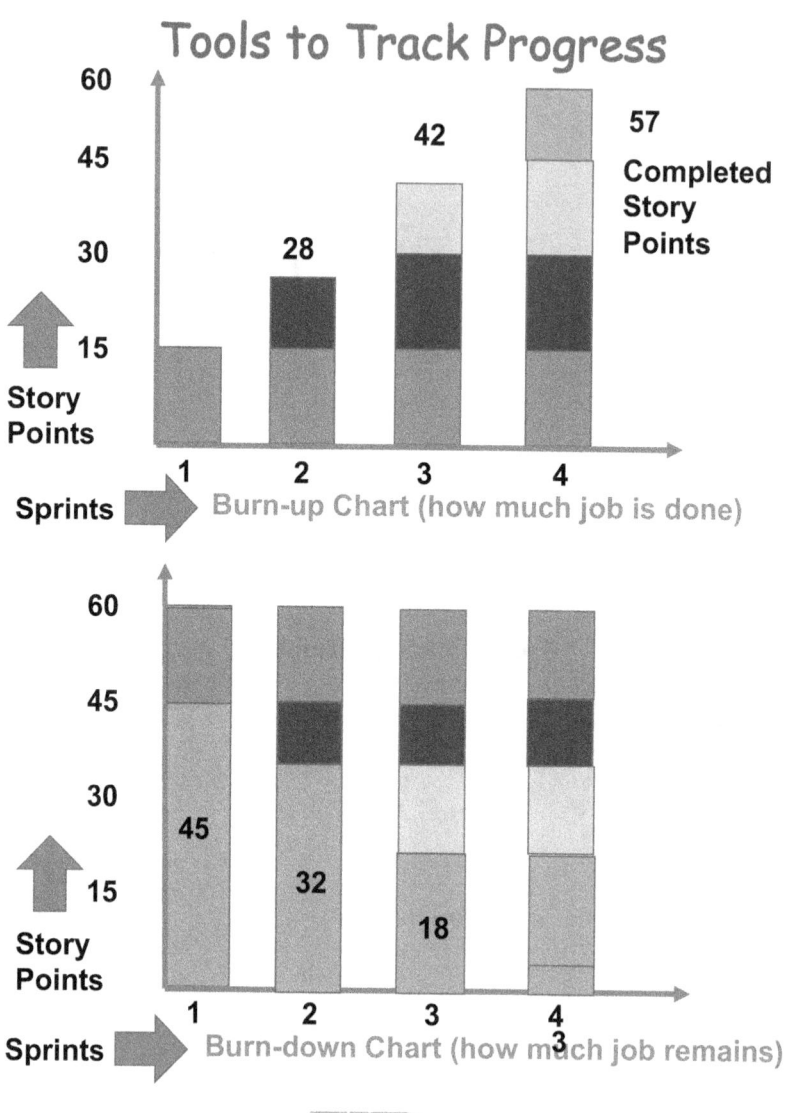

www.ingramcontent.com/pod-product-compliance
Lightning Source LLC
Chambersburg PA
CBHW071119220526
45467CB00004B/1963